ANCIENT ROME

A Book to Begin On

ANCIENT ROME

by SOPHIA HARVATI FENTON

illustrated by RICHARD CUFFARI

HOLT, RINEHART AND WINSTON
New York   Chicago   San Francisco

BOOKS BY SOPHIA HARVATI FENTON

Ancient Egypt, A Book to Begin On
Ancient Rome, A Book to Begin On
Greece, A Book to Begin On

This book is dedicated to my mother,
Athena Kondraki Harvati

About three thousand years ago there was a small village that grew until it conquered the whole world. This village was Rome.

The ancient Romans believed a legend that Rome was founded on the first of April in 753 B.C. by Romulus.

They also believed that Romulus was the descendant of the Trojan prince Aeneas, son of the goddess Venus. After Troy, a city in Asia, was conquered by the Greeks, Aeneas sailed to Italy. There he became the King of Latium.

More than two hundred years later, twin boys, Romulus and Remus, were born in Latium. Their mother was a great-great-granddaughter of Aeneas. Their father was the god Mars. A wicked uncle had the twins thrown into the river Tiber, and the basket with the babies in it was found by a she-wolf, who took care of them.

The boys grew up and started to build a new city. But they quarreled, and Romulus killed Remus. Then he gave his own name to the city, Rome. The she-wolf became its symbol.

That is the legend. The true story is somewhat different.

Thousands of years ago, many people lived on the long mountainous peninsula of Italy, which is connected to Europe by the Alps in the north and surrounded by the Mediterranean Sea. These people were the Ligurians, the Samnites, the Sabines, the Umbrians, the Latins.

They had come to Italy through the Alps from the east of Europe. Later, the Etruscans came by sea, probably from Asia Minor.

LIGURIA

ETRURIA

UMBRIA

Corsica

SABINES

Rome●

LATIUM

SAMNIUM

Sardinia

●Tarentum
(Greek)

MEDITERRANEAN SEA

Sicily

Carthage●

●Syracuse
(Greek)

AFRICA

Since there was no form of government in Italy, all these different people were free to settle and to build anywhere they liked.

Around 800 B.C., the Greeks began to build colonies in the south of Italy. They also settled in Sicily, the big island which lies south of the mainland.

The Carthaginians, from the north coast of Africa, settled on the western part of this same island.

The Latins had settled in the plain of Latium on the west coast of the peninsula by the river Tiber. They lived in small villages spread over the seven hills of that plain. Their neighbors to the east were the Sabines.

In order to defend themselves from invaders, the Latins and the Sabines soon formed the Latin League.

Meanwhile, the Etruscans had settled to the north of Latium. They knew many things the Latins did not know: how to build ships, roads and beautiful houses; how to make fine vases and statues. They were rich and strong. They had conquered many of the peoples who lived in Italy. Around 600 B.C., the Etruscans conquered Latium as well.

Then they united all the small villages of the seven hills and made them into one city.

This was Rome.

So far as we know, over a period of two centuries, seven kings, who were Latin, Sabine and Etruscan, ruled Rome.

Each king acted as priest, judge and general of the army.

The population of Rome was divided into two groups: the patricians and the plebeians.

Patres is the Latin word for fathers. The patricians claimed to be the descendants of the founders of the city. The elders of the patrician families formed a group that gave advice to the king. This was known as the Senate.

Plebs is the Latin word for common people. The plebeians were the newcomers. They were usually workmen, shopkeepers and traders.

Under the kings, Rome was strong and disciplined. The army defeated many of her neighbors.

The kings, especially the Etruscans, built temples to the gods, the *Circus Maximus* (Great Arena) for races and athletic contests, and a sewage system. They also fortified the city with a huge wall that enclosed the seven hills.

The last of the seven kings was Tarquin the Proud, an Etruscan. He was cruel. The Romans revolted and drove him out in 510 B.C.

This was the end of the era of kings.

Now the Senate was the only government in Rome. The Senators decided to elect two leaders among themselves. These were called *consuls*. The consuls were also the generals-in-chief of the army.

So, in 509 B.C., Rome became a republic. A republic is a government in which citizens handle the business of the country.

The new republic had to fight in order to survive. Peoples from Italy kept invading Latium. In 390 B.C., Rome had to defend itself against the Gauls. The Gauls had come across the Alps from France into Italy. The other Latin cities did not help Rome to drive back the Gauls. So the Romans decided they would be safer if they ruled the rest of the Latin League.

By 295 B.C., through conquests and alliances, Rome was the leading power of central Italy.

Within twenty years, Rome had conquered all of southern Italy and the Greek colonies as well.

The people of Tarentum, one of the rich Greek colonies, asked Pyrrhus, the King of Epirus in Greece, to come and help them against the Romans. He came with his army and his elephants. The Romans had never seen these enormous animals before, and they were terrified. Even so, they managed to kill so many of the soldiers of Pyrrhus' victorious army that the expression "Pyrrhic victory" came to mean "a victory that is not worth the losses."

While the Roman army was fighting in the south, the patricians and the plebeians were fighting each other in Rome.

The patricians had all the power. They were the only ones who could be senators, consuls, priests and judges.

The plebeians had none of the rights the patricians had, even though they were also Roman citizens and served in the army. What was worse, they could easily become slaves if they did not pay their debts. They decided to demand the same rights as the patricians.

In 494 B.C., the plebeians went on strike. They refused to work or to serve as soldiers.

Rome was at war then. She needed their help. So

the Senate came to an agreement with the plebeians: No longer would any plebeian be enslaved for debts. Those already enslaved would be freed. There would be two magistrates, called "tribunes," elected by the plebeians to protect their interests in the Senate.

Until then, unwritten laws allowed the patricians to decide justice for themselves. In 451 B.C., as a result of the plebeian uprising, Twelve Tables with written laws were set up for all to see in the Forum, the public meeting place.

In 287 B.C., all Roman citizens were given equal rights. This was a great victory for the plebeians and gave new strength to a united Rome.

By this time most of Italy belonged to Rome.

The senators sent governors to the conquered places. They decided on the amount of the taxes that were to be paid. They established the laws of Rome all over Italy.

They also gave land in the new territory to Romans who did not own any. These colonists helped make the rest of Italy Roman and to spread the Latin language.

It was not long before all the conquered peoples felt that they were part of one state. The Romans were the first to create the idea of one state.

"Rome's power," said the great orator and political figure, Cicero, "was born, increased and maintained through the Roman religion."

The Romans were very religious. They believed in many gods. Jupiter was the father of the gods, Juno was his wife. Minerva was the goddess of wisdom, Mars, the god of war. Most of these gods were taken from the Etruscan and Greek religions.

Before taking any action, the Romans consulted the *augur*. The augur was a man who was supposed to be able to read the will of the gods through signs such as the flight of birds.

Besides the gods all the Romans believed in, every family worshiped the spirits of its ancestors, called *Lares*, and many other spirits that protected the house, called *Penates*.

The family religious ceremonies were performed by the father.

JUPITER JUNO MINERVA MARS

The father—in Latin, *pater familias*—was the absolute master of all his household. He even could have any member of his family put to death.

The mother—in Latin, *matrona*—was very much respected by everyone. She took care of the children. She handled the servants in the house. She helped the father with advice in his activities. She also attended public ceremonies and spectacles with him.

Even so the mother was responsible to the father, as was everyone else. The boys were still responsible to him even when they were old enough to vote.

No one ever thought of disobeying the father. Strict discipline was the rule in every Roman family.

The father was his children's first teacher. He taught them to read and write and count. All the children had to learn by heart the Twelve Tables of the written laws.

Senators took their sons when they were seven or eight years old to the Senate where they could listen to the discussions of matters of state.

Around 250 B.C., schools were established. Boys went there accompanied by a slave, who was usually an educated Greek and was called a pedagogue. Pedagogue is from a Greek word; it means "children's educator."

In later times, girls also went to school.

The Roman house was a simple, square building. In the beginning, it had only one room, called the *atrium*. Later, it had more rooms which were built around the atrium.

The food was as simple as the house. The Romans ate barley bread, boiled vegetables, cheese, olives, figs, and they drank wine. Meat was a rare treat reserved for holidays.

Men's everyday dress was a plain tunic. The *toga*, made of white wool, was the official outfit for attending state and religious ceremonies.

The *stola*, a belted dress, was worn by women. When they went out in public with their husbands, they wrapped a large, long scarf around the stola.

The Senate, the government of Rome, was formed by citizens who had already served as generals, consuls or magistrates. So they already had great experience in state matters.

In the early days of the republic, the senators were devoted to Rome's interests. For them nothing came before their country.

In times of danger for the city the Senate appointed one man as a *dictator*. For a period of no more than six months, the dictator controlled the army and the public affairs.

Cincinnatus, appointed dictator in 458 B.C., led the Roman army to safety when it was about to be slaughtered by the enemy. Sixteen days after his nomination, when the city was safe, Cincinnatus resigned.

In later times the dictators used their absolute power to hurt Rome.

By 300 B.C., the Roman army was well organized. Every citizen served in it except those people who owned no property.

The basic unit of the army was the *legion*, made up of 4500 soldiers. The discipline of the legions was excellent.

The legions kept the provinces under control. They could move easily on the direct roads that had been built by the Roman engineers to connect the rest of the country with Rome. In those days the saying, "All roads lead to Rome" was actually true.

By 264 B.C., the Romans had conquered the Greek colonies in the south of Italy. Then they fought the Carthaginians in Sicily. In 262 B.C., the Punic Wars began.

The wars were called "Punic" because *Poeni* (*puni*) is the Latin word for Phoenicians. The Carthaginians were Phoenicians. They had come from the coast of Syria to northern Africa. There they built the great city of Carthage. Skillful sailors and traders, they were the greatest sea power of those times. They controlled the trade on the seas around Sicily and the western Mediterranean. They were serious rivals to the Roman trade. The Romans did not feel safe.

The Punic Wars went on, with interruptions, for over one hundred years. Rome itself was almost captured by the great Carthaginian general, Hannibal.

In the end the Romans won. Their fleet was strong enough to sail to Africa and fight the enemy in Carthage itself. The Romans did not feel safe until, in 149 B.C., they had completely wiped out the beautiful city of Carthage.

In the same year Greece also became a Roman province. The King of Macedon was an ally of Carthage. So the Romans attacked Greece and took it over after they had defeated Carthage.

Now nothing could stand in the way of Rome's conquests. By the first century B.C., the Romans were able to call the whole Mediterranean *mare nostrum* which means "our sea."

STURGEON HEIGHTS SCHOOL
7006

Great wealth and many slaves now came pouring into Rome from all the conquered countries.

Officials, generals and traders had become very rich. But many people had gained nothing; small farmers and workers could not make a living.

Two brothers, Tiberius Gracchus (elected tribune in 133 B.C.) and Gaius Gracchus (elected tribune in 121 B.C.), tried to help the poor by changing some laws. Gaius succeeded to some extent. But both of them were assassinated.

This struggle between the rich and the poor was in fact the beginning of the end of the Roman republic.

The end of the republic was hastened when the Roman army became an army of professionals: citizens who stayed on in the army and made it their life's work. This was brought about by a general named Marius, elected consul in 100 B.C. From then on the soldiers listened less to the Senate and more to the generals who paid them. The generals urged their men to victory with promises of loot and land, as well as more pay.

It was the general, Sulla, in 82 B.C., who brought the Roman army against Rome. Sulla, as dictator, treated Rome like any other conquered city. He put thousands of people to death.

After him, many other generals did the same thing when the laws of Rome did not please them.

The generals had become the real rulers of Rome.

Though they kept conquering new provinces, they also fought with each other. Every general wanted to rule Rome.

Gaius Julius Caesar, born in 101 B.C., was one of the greatest generals who ever lived. He conquered France and most of Europe as far north as England. The senators grew afraid of his strength. They ordered him to disband his legions. Caesar refused. Instead he brought his army back to Italy in defiance of the Senators and their favorite general, Pompey.

Pompey fled to Greece, where Caesar defeated him in 48 B.C.

Then, for three years, Caesar extended his power all over the lands bordering the Mediterranean Sea.

Caesar went back to Rome in 46 B.C. as dictator.

It was the custom for victorious generals to enter the city in a triumphal parade. Caesar's was one of the most splendid Rome had ever seen. His chariot was accompanied by countless carts loaded with captured gold and works of art. Thousands of slaves from Spain, France, Greece, Asia and Africa walked behind him.

In 44 B.C., Caesar was made dictator for life by the Senate. His power was unlimited. His genius for ruling had already shown itself. He organized the administration of the provinces. He lowered taxes. He gave land to the poor. He even established the Julian Calendar, the one we still use today.

But some Romans, and among them some of his friends, came to believe that Caesar planned to end the republic and make himself King of Rome.

In March, that same year, they murdered him.

The men who killed Caesar thought that they had saved the republic. But they were too late.

Caesar's assassination was followed by a civil war. It was actually another fight among the generals. Octavian, Caesar's heir, overcame all his adversaries. At the battle of Actium in Greece (31 B.C.), he defeated the last of his enemies, the general, Mark Antony, and Cleopatra, the Queen of Egypt. She had helped Mark Antony fight with her warships. So Egypt became another Roman province.

Octavian remained the sole master of the Roman Empire.

Caesar's murder had been a lesson to Octavian in how to use unlimited power with wisdom.

Therefore, in 27 B.C., he announced that the Senate and the people were the true rulers of the Empire. He did not really mean this, but it was the only way to keep the Romans calm and to be able to rule as he wished.

The people of Rome were wild with joy. They gave him the title of "Emperor Caesar Augustus," which meant "the highest military leader, the descendant of gods and the highest religious authority."

With Octavian, the period of the Roman Empire began.

The Emperor Augustus, as Octavian is known in history, did not enlarge the Empire. He only tried to protect its boundaries from invaders.

After so many centuries of war, peace finally came to Rome.

Augustus spent his time organizing his vast Empire. His reign is known as the Augustan Age, during which order and security were established.

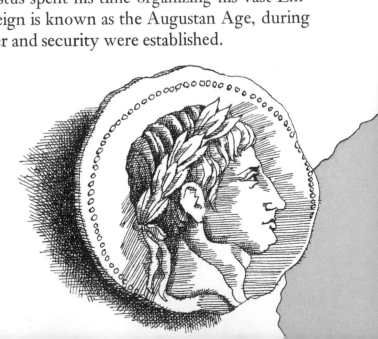

BLACK SEA

Rome

MEDITERRANEAN SEA

THE ROMAN EMPIRE
AT THE TIME OF AUGUSTUS

Rome ruled the world. On the site of Romulus's small village a splendid city stood, filled with temples, forums, public baths, marble houses, statues and paintings.

Works of art were shipped to Rome from Greece and the countries from the east. Thousands of educated Greeks were brought to Italy as slaves. Among them was Polybius, who taught the Romans that history books should be based on facts and not mythology.

Thus, by conquering the peoples of the east, the Romans learned to appreciate luxuries and education. A Roman was not thought of as learned unless he spoke Greek as well as Latin.

Great Latin writers lived in Augustus's time: Virgil, who wrote the *Aeneid*, the long story-poem about the founding of Rome; the poets, Horace and Ovid; the historian, Livy.

During the reign of Augustus a baby was born in the Roman province of Palestine. His name was Jesus.

Rome in the days of Augustus was crowded with poor people. They existed on the "bread and circuses" that the Emperor gave them.

It was the ruler's duty to provide free entertainment for the people. This Augustus did lavishly. Romans flocked to the cruel contests that took place in the *Circus Maximus*. Slaves fought with wild animals, or slaves fought each other to the death. These slaves were the famous gladiators.

The Romans also loved the theater. They enjoyed the comedies of Plautus. The plays were about everyday happenings in Rome. They also poked fun at affairs of state. Plautus learned to be a playwright by studying the Greek comedies. His heroes were supposed to be Greeks. It was a clever way of getting the Romans to laugh at their own manners and their own government. That way Plautus also made sure that the Roman state could not accuse him of laughing at it.

NERO

In Augustus's time the ethics of the Romans changed greatly. The father had lost his authority. Family ties were weakened. Senators cared more about their own interests than those of the nation. Everyone sought pleasure at any cost. There was no respect for religious or moral laws.

Augustus tried hard to bring back the old, simple, religious way of life. But he did not succeed.

Augustus died in 14 A.D. Some of the emperors who followed him are known to history as monsters. Caligula, for instance, wanted his horse to be given the honors of a consul. Nero executed many people, among them his own mother. No one felt safe any more.

But beginning in 69 A.D., the emperors of the Flavian and then those of the Antonine families brought order, peace and unity back to the Empire. Marcus Aurelius, one of the Antonines, believed that men exist to help one another.

Commodus, the last of the Antonines, was cruel and incapable of ruling. The Empire was ready to fall apart.

In the midst of this decay, the new religion of Jesus Christ sprang up among the people. It preached love and brotherhood. Those who followed the new religion were called "Christians." They were persecuted with the utmost cruelty because they refused to worship the emperors and the old Roman gods.

Beginning in 268, the Emperors from the frontier province of Illyria brought order back to the Empire.

The Emperor Constantine built a new Rome in the east, on the site of a Greek colony called Byzantium. He named this city after himself, calling it Constantinople.

Constantine changed the history of the world when he proclaimed that "every man is to be allowed to practice whatever religion he chooses." This was the *Edict of Milan*, put forth in 313. It put an end to the persecution of the Christians. By 392, Christianity had become the state religion of the Roman Empire.

Theodosius I, in 395, divided the Empire into two parts; each was ruled by one of his sons. Rome was the capital of the west, Constantinople of the east.

Meanwhile, tribes from Asia were pushing toward Europe. Many of them broke through the boundaries of the Empire and took pieces of it for themselves. Finally Rome itself fell to the Vandals in 476.

This date is considered the end of the Roman Empire in the west.

The eastern Roman Empire kept driving back the invaders for many centuries. But since the end of the fourth century its ties with Rome had been growing weaker. Constantinople became, in time, the center of a new Christian world known as the Byzantine Empire.

When Constantinople finally fell to the Turks in 1453, it was the end of the Roman Empire in the east.

Though its Empire fell many centuries ago, Rome is still alive.

Many of her great buildings, her circuses, her theaters, aqueducts and roads still exist. Modern engineers and architects often use them as models for today's construction.

Millions of people today speak Italian, French, Spanish, Portugese and Rumanian. These languages have all sprung directly from Latin.

The greatest achievement of the Romans was their laws.

It was Justinian, an emperor of the eastern Roman Empire, who ordered the many Roman laws to be recorded with order and clarity.

And so, in 533, the *Corpus Juris Civilis* was published. We call it "civil law." Even today it is used as a guide for justice for all men, everywhere.

The Romans had learned science, philosophy (love of wisdom) and the arts from the conquered peoples.

They put this knowledge into useful achievements because they had practical minds. They realized the dream of the Greek philosophers and Alexander the Great: They created a united state, a universal community, formed of many peoples of different faiths and races.

We still live in nations based on the Roman idea of the "state."

"Law," the Romans taught the world, "is the art of the good and the fair . . ."

"Justice is the constant and perpetual will to give each man his right." (*Digest of Justinian*).

ABOUT THE AUTHOR

Sophia Harvati Fenton is a distinguished Greek child psychologist and educator, and the author of *Greece, ABTBO* and *Ancient Egypt, ABTBO*. She and her husband, author and translator Edward Fenton, divide their time between their home in Washington, D.C. and a second home in Mrs. Fenton's native Greece.

ABOUT THE ARTIST

Richard Cuffari, a graduate of Pratt Institute, has illustrated more than forty books for young people. He has a great interest in antiquity and does much of his research from an extensive personal library. Mr. Cuffari lives with his family in Brooklyn, New York.

ABOUT THE BOOK

The drawings for this book were done in fine line and wash. For his second color, Mr. Cuffari chose Pompeian red, a color that was dominant in the art of ancient Rome and still evokes a feeling of the period. The text was set in Janson, with Augustea display type. The book was printed by offset.